DATE DUE

American Lives

George W. Bush

Rick Burke

Heinemann Library
Chicago, Illinois

Created by the publishing team
at Heinemann Library

Designed by Ginkgo Creative, Inc.
Photo Research by Kathryn Creech
Printed and Bound in the United States by
Lake Book Manufacturing, Inc.

07 06 05 04
10 9 8 7 6 5 4 3 2

Library of Congress Cataloging-in-Publication Data
Burke, Rick, 1957-
  George W. Bush / Rick Burke.
     p. cm. — (American lives)
Summary: A biography of the former Texas
governor who was elected president in the much-
contested presidential race of 2000.
Includes bibliographical references and index.
  ISBN 1-40340-157-8 ((lib. bdg.)) —
  ISBN 1-40340-413-5 ((pbk.))
  1. Bush, George W. (George Walker), 1946—
Juvenile literature. 2. Presidents—United States—
Biography—Juvenile literature. [1. George W.
(George Walker), 1946-. 2. Presidents.] I. Title.
  E903 .B87 2002
  973.931'092—dc21

                        2002004558

Acknowledgments
The author and publishers are grateful to the
following for permission to reproduce copyright
material: pp. 4L, 6, 7, 8, 12, 13 George Bush
Library; p. 4R White House Photo; p. 5 Kenneth
Lambert/AP/Wide World Photos; p. 9 Darren
McCollester/Getty Images; p. 10 AFP/Corbis; p. 11
Bettmann/Corbis; p. 14 Mark Elias/AP/Wide World
Photos; p. 15 Angel Franco/The New York Times;
p. 16 AP/Wide World Photos; pp. 17, 18, 29 David
Woo; p. 20 Jeff Mitchell/Reuters/Corbis; p. 22 Jim
Bourg/Reuters/Corbis; p. 23 Paul Morse/White
House Photo; p. 24 Spencer Platt/Getty Images;
p. 25 Alex Wong/Getty Images; p. 26 William
Philpott/Reuters/Corbis; p. 27 Eric Draper/White
House Photo; p. 28 Chuck Kennedy/KRT/Tribune
Media Services

Cover photograph: AFP/Corbis

Special thanks to Patrick Halladay for his help in
the preparation of this book. Rick Burke thanks the
Carpenter family . . . thanks for everything.

Every effort has been made to contact copyright
holders of any material reproduced in this book.
Any omissions will be rectified in subsequent
printings if notice is given to the publisher.

Some words are shown in bold, **like this.** You can
find out what they mean by looking in the glossary.

On this book's cover, George W. Bush is talking to workers
at a printing company in Maryland on October 24, 2001.

Contents

Father and Son

On January 20, 2001, George Walker Bush became the 43rd president of the United States and made history. Bush's father, George Herbert Walker Bush, was the nation's 41st president from 1989 to 1993.

The only other father and son to be elected to the country's highest office were John Adams and his son John Quincy Adams. John was the second United States president and John Quincy was the sixth.

These photos of George W. Bush, left, and his father, right, were taken in the White House.

Bush likes to spend time at his ranch in Texas.

Bush had always wanted to be like his father. He respected him and thought he had been successful in life and as a president. Bush wanted to do as good of a job as his dad did.

Becoming president of the United States and being a good president are probably two of the hardest things to do in the world. Bush also wanted to be a good president like his father was. It wouldn't be easy.

Bush Firsts

- *First son of a president to be elected president since 1825.*
- *First president with a **master's degree** in business.*
- *First president to have played Little League baseball.*

Growing Up

George W. Bush was born on July 6, 1946, in New Haven, Connecticut. He was the first child his parents had. His father was going to college at Yale University in New Haven when George was born. His father was able to finish college in just two and a half years. Most people take four years.

After George's father finished college, the Bush family moved to Texas because his father wanted to work in the oil business. George was two years old. He spent most of his childhood in Midland, Texas.

George is wearing his baseball uniform in this picture from 1954.

The Life of George W. Bush

1946	1968	1975	1977
Born on July 6 in New Haven, Connecticut.	**Graduated** from Yale.	Graduated from Harvard.	Married Laura Welch.

The Bushes had five other children besides George. His brothers and sisters were Robin, Dorothy, Neil, Marvin, and John, who was called Jeb.

When George was seven years old, his sister Robin died. His parents were very sad. George made it his job to make his parents feel happy again. He told them jokes and tried to cheer them up.

George, seen here standing and wearing a white shirt, is ten years old in this photo.

1988	1988	1994	2000
Helped with his father's presidential **campaign.**	*Bought the Texas Rangers.*	*Elected* **governor** *of Texas.*	*Elected president of the United States.*

School

George wasn't the best student at school, but he had a lot of friends and liked to have fun. He played baseball and kept track of how many hits and home runs that **professional** baseball players had. When he was growing up, George said he would rather be Willie Mays, the famous baseball player, than the president.

George liked to make other people laugh, too. Once, George was sent to the principal's office for drawing a beard on his own face. He got spanked three times with a wooden paddle.

George was a cheerleader at Phillips Academy. This picture is from 1964.

George played on the school baseball team in his first year at Yale University.

His parents moved to Houston, Texas, and after a few years, George went away to school at Phillips Academy in Andover, Massachusetts. George played baseball and basketball on the school's teams and also became the head cheerleader.

Like his father, George went to college at Yale University, where his father had been an excellent student. In 1968, George **graduated** from Yale after four years of going to school.

Yale Years

George was just an OK student at Yale. In a speech he gave at Yale in 2001, he made fun of the grades he got during college.

National Guard and Harvard

When George finished at Yale, the United States was in a war in the country of Vietnam. American men who were George's age were being picked to fight in the war. George joined the **National Guard.** He learned how to fly an airplane and became a fighter pilot like his father was in World War II.

George was never asked to fight in the war, but he was ready to serve. He flew a plane called the F-102, which was a jet that had room for just the pilot.

George's father was with George when he joined the National Guard in 1968.

George and Texas

When he was at Harvard, George really missed Texas. He liked to wear his cowboy boots and pilot jacket to show where he was from.

Dorothy   Jeb   George Jr.   George   Barbara   Marvin   Neil

After he left the National Guard in 1973, George worked for the **Professional** United Leadership League, which helped poor African-American boys in Houston. He liked working with the boys and trying to make their lives better. Once, when a boy came to the center without shoes, George went out and bought him a pair.

George went back to school in 1973. He went to Harvard University in Cambridge, Massachusetts, to get a **master's degree.** After he got his degree, George decided to go back to Texas. He wanted to work in the oil business, like his father did.

11

Laura

Two important things happened to George in 1977. He tried to be elected to **Congress** like his father had been, and he fell in love.

George wanted the voters of west Texas to send him to Washington, D.C. He wanted to serve as a government leader in Congress. He started to **campaign** to get people to vote for him.

George and Laura are shown here with family members on their wedding day, November 5, 1977, in Midland, Texas.

During the campaign, George went to a party at a friend's house and met Laura Welch, a school librarian. George and Laura had gone to junior high school together in Midland, Texas, but they didn't really know each other. They went on a date the next night to play miniature golf.

Laura helped George with his campaign in 1978.

Three months later, they were married. They didn't go on a vacation after their wedding so that George could keep campaigning. In 1981, Laura gave birth to twin daughters. They were named Jenna and Barbara after their grandmothers.

Neighbors

George and Laura lived in different apartments in the same building in Houston, Texas. But they never saw each other until they met in Midland a few years later.

Father's Victory

George won when it came to love, but he lost the election to **Congress.** He decided to start his own oil company called Arbusto, which means "bush" in Spanish.

The company's workers tried to find oil and gas under the fields of Texas, but they weren't very lucky. They didn't find much oil or gas. Another company bought Arbusto, however. This gave George a chance to get into **politics,** something he thought he would be good at.

Along with the **governor** of Texas, George celebrated his father being named as a **candidate** in the 1988 election.

George and Laura are seen here in Washington, D.C., on the day George's father became president.

George's father was the vice president of the United States from 1981 to 1989. Ronald Reagan, the president during those years, was done serving as president. George's father wanted to take his place.

George moved his family to Washington, D.C., to help with his father's presidential **campaign.** With George's help, his father defeated Michael Dukakis in November 1988. His father became the nation's 41st president.

Another Presidential Family

The Harrison family also had two family members become presidents. William Henry Harrison was the ninth president, but he died 31 days after starting his **term.** *His grandson, Benjamin Harrison, was the 23rd president.*

Texas Rangers

Instead of staying in Washington and working for his father, George moved back to Texas. He wanted to do something he had always dreamed about when he was a child. In 1988, George sold his part of the oil company and used the money to buy the Texas Rangers baseball team.

George loved being in the world of **professional** baseball. He was a fan of the game, but he was a good owner, too.

In April 1989, George talked to reporters after it was announced that he was buying the Rangers.

George the Athlete

George likes to stay in good shape. He tries to run and exercise at least one hour a day.

George talked to baseball player Nolan Ryan while George was the team's owner.

Instead of sitting in a private area, George liked to sit with the rest of the fans and talk about baseball. He was able to get a new stadium built for the team in Arlington, Texas. George helped design the stadium.

Barbara Bush, George's mother, went to Texas to throw out the first pitch before a Rangers game. She brought one of her dog's puppies with her to give to George's family. The dog's name was Spot, and he followed George everywhere.

Governor

In 1992, George's father wanted to be elected president again, but Bill Clinton defeated him. George was hurt by his father's loss. George W. Bush decided then that he wanted to be elected **governor** of Texas.

Being the owner of the Texas Rangers had made him popular with the people of the state. In 1994, Bush **campaigned** against Texas Governor Ann Richards. It was a close election, but George W. Bush won. He became only the second **Republican** governor in Texas in more than 125 years.

George shared the stage with his family on November 8, 1994, the night he won the election to be the governor of Texas.

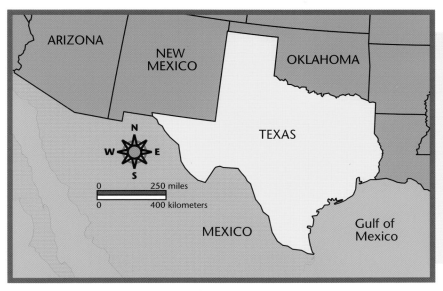

Texas is the second-biggest state in the nation. About 576,000 people voted for Bush in the 1998 election for governor.

Right away, Bush was able to do something that other governors couldn't get done. He made sure more money was spent for Texas schools. Bush wanted all children to have a chance to learn. He had students from the state take tests every year to see how much they had learned. The voters of Texas liked what Bush had done. They reelected him in 1998 to another four years as governor.

Laura's Speeches

During the campaign, George promised Laura that she would never have to speak in front of crowds because Laura was shy. However, she did have to speak to a crowd a few months later because George couldn't make it. Laura soon became a good speaker.

2000 Campaign

Being the owner of the Texas Rangers made Bush well-known in the state of Texas. Being the **governor** of Texas made Bush well-known and popular with many people throughout the United States.

Bush tried to get elected president in 2000. He was the **candidate** for the **Republican Party.** Bill Clinton's vice president, Al Gore, was the candidate for the **Democratic Party.**

Bush and the candidate for vice president, Richard Cheney, are seen here on a campaign stop in Wyoming in 2000.

During the **campaign,** the voters of the United States got to see and hear both candidates talk many times. Bush looked friendly and relaxed when he spoke to crowds. Some people thought that Gore had a harder time speaking to crowds.

The 2000 presidential election was one of the closest in the history of the United States. Gore received more votes than Bush, but by the end of Election Day, there was no winner. Neither Bush nor Gore had enough **electoral votes.**

This map shows the states that each candidate won in the election.

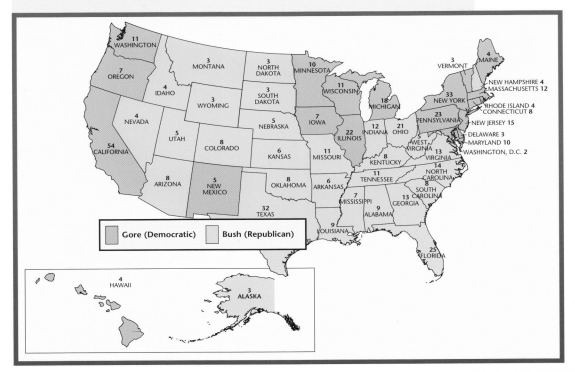

President

To be elected president, one of the **candidates** needed 270 **electoral votes.** Each state has a certain number of electoral votes. Whoever gets the most votes from a state's **citizens** gets all of the state's electoral votes. By the end of Election Day, Gore had 255 electoral votes. Bush had 246. Florida's votes still had to be counted.

Finally, Florida was counted, and its 25 electoral votes were given to Bush. That gave Bush 271 votes. He won the election.

Bush's first day as president was January 20, 2001. His daughters and wife are at his side in this picture.

Bush visited these kids at their school in Connecticut in April 2001.

There were many things that Bush wanted to change in the United States. He wanted to lower the taxes that people paid to help run the government in the United States. He also wanted to have the government give more tests to students. Bush thought this was a good way to make sure that every child got a good education.

Political Family

*Other Bush family members have served in the government. Prescott Bush, George's grandfather, was a government leader from Connecticut. George's brother Jeb was the **governor** of Florida.*

He wanted to be the best president he could be. He told Americans, "I will work to earn your respect."

America Under Attack

One of the saddest days in the history of the United States was September 11, 2001. That morning, Bush was at a school in Florida visiting students. One of his helpers told him something terrible had happened.

That morning, **terrorists** took over four jet airplanes from the pilots. Three planes crashed into buildings. Two of the planes hit the twin towers of the World Trade Center in New York City. The third crashed into the Pentagon in Washington, D.C. The Pentagon is where the United States Army, Navy, Air Force, and Marines all have their headquarters.

When a plane hit the second tower, there was an explosion. The towers fell to the ground later in the day.

The fourth plane didn't crash into a large building because the passengers fought with the terrorists. However, the plane did crash into a field in Pennsylvania.

The Secret Service, the men and women who protect the president, had Bush get on a plane and fly around the country so he wouldn't be a target for the terrorists. In a way, Bush was leading the country from the sky.

The plane crash at the Pentagon caused a huge fire.

Bush's Message

Bush made a statement from the Barksdale Air Force Base in Louisiana after the attack. He said, "Make no mistake, the United States will hunt down and punish those responsible for these cowardly acts."

War on Terrorism

The crashes killed thousands of people. The people of the United States watched the film of the planes crashing into the buildings and cried. Bush was sad, too, but he knew the country needed him to tell them what they needed to do.

President Bush told the people of the United States and the world that his nation would not accept being attacked by **terrorists** without a fight. He also told the countries that were helping terrorists that they had to stop.

Bush visited firefighters and other workers at the World Trade Center site three days after the attacks.

The president said that the other countries of the world were either with the United States and against terrorism, or they were enemies of the United States.

On October 7, 2001, the United States attacked the country of Afghanistan because that country allowed terrorists to be free and kill innocent people. Bush promised that the United States would keep fighting until terrorism was just a bad memory.

Bush announced in a television speech that the United States had begun an attack on Afghanistan.

Bush's Future

George W. Bush has done things in life a lot like his father did. He went to the same schools and played the same sports. When the United States went to war, he became a fighter pilot like his father. George entered the same business as his dad and also followed his father's lead by getting into **politics.** He was elected to the presidency just eight years after his father left the office.

Bush gave a speech at the White House on March 11, 2002, six months after the attacks. He said that the war on terrorism had to continue.

When **terrorists** attacked New York City and Washington, D.C., George's courage gave the country the strength to face its enemies. No one knew how long the war against terrorism would last. But most **citizens** of the United States believed that George could lead them through the difficult times.

No one knew what the future would bring. But looking at the way President Bush handled the nation's problems in his first year as president, a lot of people thought the future was bright.

Bush was the first president to see an attack on the United States since World War II.

Glossary

campaign series of events in which candidates try to get elected

candidate person who wants to be elected

citizen person who belongs to a country

Congress part of U.S. government that makes the laws

Democratic Party one of the two major political parties in the United States. A group of people who think alike and feel the same way about ideas.

electoral vote vote that is chosen by each state to elect the president of the United States

governor leader of state government

graduate to complete a course of study at a school or college

master's degree advanced college degree

National Guard army controlled by many states

politics activities and methods in government business

professional describing an activity or job that someone does to make money and earn a living

Republican Party one of the two major political parties in the United States. A group of people who think alike and feel the same way about ideas.

term number of years that a president serves. Four years is the length of a president's term.

terrorist person who uses violence and breaks the law to try to get what he or she wants from the government

More Books to Read

Bredeson, Carmen. *George W. Bush: The 43rd President.* Berkeley Heights, N.J.: Enslow Publishers, 2002.

Marsh, Carole. *George W. Bush: America's Newest President and His White House Family.* Peachtree City, Ga.: Gallopade International, 2001.

Places to Visit

Texas Rangers Ballpark
1000 Ballpark Way
Arlington, TX 76011
Visitor Information: (817) 273-5222

The White House
1600 Pennsylvania Avenue NW
Washington, D.C. 20500
Visitor Information: (202) 456-7041

World Trade Center Site
Church Street
(between Liberty and Vesey Streets)
New York, NY

Index